Only A Star

WRITTEN BY

Margery Facklam

ILLUSTRATED BY

Nancy Carpenter

WILLIAM B. EERDMANS PUBLISHING COMPANY, INC.

Grand Rapids, Michigan • Cambridge, U.K.

Copyright © 1996 Wm. B. Eerdmans Publishing Co.
255 Jefferson Ave., S.E., Grand Rapids, Michigan 49503
P.O. Box 163, Cambridge CB3 9PU U.K.

Printed in Hong Kong

00 99 98 97 96   7 6 5 4 3 2 1

Library of Congress Cataloging-in-Publication Data
Facklam, Margery.
Only a star / by Margery Facklam ; illustrated by Nancy Carpenter.
[32] p. cm. col ill
Summary: A poem describing the star that was present at the first Christmas.
ISBN 0-8028-5122-3
1. Children's poetry, American. 2. Star of Bethlehem— Juvenile poetry.
3. Christmas — Juvenile poetry.   [1. Star of Bethlehem — Poetry.
2. Jesus Christ — Nativity — Poetry. 3. American poetry.]
I. Carpenter, Nancy. ill.   II. Title
JP
FACKLAN   PS3556.A278054   1996
811'.54— dc20   96-1420
CIP
AC

Designed by Joy Chu

For Katherine Anne Thomas,
who asked the question that became this book.
And in joyful memory of my brother,
David Metz. — M.F.

For Jack and Donna. — N.C.

What were the trimmings
that first Christmas morning?

What brightened the stable
to welcome the Child?
Only a Star.

But it glistened on dewdrops and
turned them to diamonds.
Spidery threads became ribbons of silk.

Even the hay in the hard,
wooden manger
gleamed satin-soft
surrounding the Babe.

A dragonfly hovered on wings of clear crystal scattering the light in a rainbow of gems.

A scurrying scarab caught in the starglow
added an emerald to trim the Child's bed.

Doves preened
feathers drifted,
like guardian angels
on watch overhead.

Tired from its journey,
a donkey stood silent.
Its worn copper bell glowed
like gold for a King.

Three chubby jerboas danced
in the starlight —
a ritual of joy for this holy day.

A snail left a trail that glittered like tinsel.
Dust sparkled in banners of heavenly light.

Cradled by down in the nest of a nightingale,
eggs became ornaments made for this birth.

What trimmed the stable
that first Christmas morning?

Only a Star,
but it dazzled the earth.

More about the Animals

All the little creatures that brightened the stable in this story lived in the Holy Land when Christ was born, and they live there still.

ORB-WEB SPIDER

More than 3,500 kinds of orb-web spiders spin their silken webs in hidden corners of the world — in gardens, attics, stables, or anywhere they might catch insects. Many people believe it's bad luck to kill a spider or break a web. A book of folklore written in 1866 suggests that this belief began because ". . . when our Blessed Lord lay in the manger, the spider spun a beautiful web, which protected the innocent Babe."

DRAGONFLY

Several different kinds of dragonflies live in the Holy Land. These big insects are carnivores that hunt for other insects during daylight hours, but they might have come awake in the brilliant light of the Christmas Star. In many cultures, the dragonfly is a symbol of renewal and rebirth.

SCARAB BEETLE

All scarab beetles are scavengers that eat dead animals. They are an important part of the world's clean-up crew on every continent except Antarctica. Despite their lowly work, scarab beetles are beautifully colored in shimmery metallic shades of blue, green, purple, bronze, and gold.

DOVE

Long before the birth of Christ, people had begun to domesticate wild rock doves. They raised these birds for food and also trained them to carry messages back to their home roosts. Doves have been symbols of peace, love, and loyalty for thousands of years.

DONKEY

More than 6,000 years ago, small wild donkeys of North Africa were domesticated, and these sturdy, reliable animals have carried people and supplies ever since. At the time of Christ's birth, wealthy people may have owned camels, but it's more likely that Mary rode on a donkey, while Joseph walked beside her as they tried to find a room for the night.

JERBOA

A jerboa is a close cousin to the gerbil. Sometimes it's called a desert rat. As it hops and leaps on its strong hind legs, with its long tail held out for balance, a jerboa looks like a tiny kangaroo. Jerboas stay in their burrows during the heat of the day, but venture out at dusk to look for food. At the Metropolitan Museum of Art in New York City, there is a small sculpture of three jerboas made by an artist about 2,000 years before the birth of Christ. The note on it says: "These tiny creatures inhabit Egypt's desert fringe, where on moonlit nights they can be seen dancing in groups."

SNAIL

Land snails in the Middle East rest during the heat of the day, but when the dew is on the ground at night, they come out to eat plants. Some kinds of land snails stay underground throughout the long, dry summers, and come out only when the ground gets wet with the first autumn rains. But all snails leave a shiny silvery trail behind them as they slide along on their one foot.

NIGHTINGALE

The nightingale is one of the songbirds mentioned in the Bible. Of all the members of the thrush family, nightingales are most famous for their flutelike, melodious songs. Most birds sing only during the day, but the male nightingale sings his most beautiful songs at night.